Robert Lima

Writers on My Watch

Poems

© 2020 Robert Lima
Printed in the United States of America

All rights reserved. This publication is protected by Copyright, and permission should be obtained from the publisher prior to any prohibited reproduction, storage in a retrieval system, or transmission in any form or by any means, electronic, mechanical, photocopying, recording, or likewise.

Published by Mt. Nittany Press, an imprint of Eifrig Publishing,
PO Box 66, Lemont, PA 16851.
Knobelsdorffstr. 44, 14059 Berlin, Germany

For information regarding permission, write to:
Rights and Permissions Department,
Eifrig Publishing,
PO Box 66, Lemont, PA 16851, USA.
permissions@eifrigpublishing.com, 888-340-6543.

Library of Congress Cataloging-in-Publication Data

LIma, Robert, Writers on My Watch: Poems
      p.   cm.

Paperback: ISBN 978-1-63233-243-1

     1. Poetry
I. Lima, Robert, II. Title.

24 23 22 21 2020
5 4 3 2 1

Printed on acid-free paper. ∞

I dedicate this chapbook to the memory of Paul West (1930-2015), Novelist, Poet, Memoirist, and Friend, who was a recognized master of the English language. I treasure the numerous autographed works of his gifted me.

R. L.

Acknowledgments:

Some of the poems in this chapbook first appeared within the prose pieces in ¡Some People! Anecdotes, Images and Letters of Persons of Interest, and others as follows:

"After an Anonymous Eighth-Century Gaelic Poet" in *Dark Lullaby. The Sandburg—Livesay Award Anthology*

"Afterwords" in *Linden Lane Magazine*

"Aphorism" in *(Borges) Simply a Man of Letters*

"Breton" in *Journal of General Education*

"Dichotomy" in *(Borges) Simply a Man of Letters*

"Dylan's Walk" in *PKP Journal / The Centre Daily Times*

"First Respects" in *Pivot*

"Gwendolyn Reading in Black Voice" in *Say that the River Turns: The Impact of Gwendolyn Brooks / Shooting Star Review*

"Horizon" in *(Borges) Simply a Man of Letters*

"Janus" in *The Chicago Literary Review / The Growth of African Literature*

"Lorca" in *Revista Romea / The Literary Review Anthology of Contemporary Latin American Literature*

"A Tomos" (formerly "Lucretius" in *Delta Epsilon Sigma Bulletin / The Literary Tabloid*)

"Randell Jarrell ..." in *Poet Lore*

"Southern Draw" in *Sandlapper. The Magazine of South Carolina*

"To William Carlos Williams: 'In Memoriam'" in *The Pittsburgh Point / Athanor / PoetryBay*

The photographs are all by the author, his wife Sally M. Lima, or are stock photos in the public domain.

The front and back covers are designed by Keith Lima.

Writers on My Watch

AMIRI BARAKA
JORGE LUIS BORGES
ANDRÉ BRETON
JOSEF BRODSKY
GWENDOLYN BROOKS
LEONARD COHEN
DEMOCRITUS
JAMES DICKEY
ROBERT FROST
FEDERICO GARCÍA LORCA
TONY HILLERMAN
RANDELL JARRELL
LEUCIPPUS
JACKSON MACLOW
HOWARD MOSS
DYLAN THOMAS
RAMON DEL VALLE-INCLAN
MARIO VARGAS LLOSA
PAUL WEST
WILLIAM CARLOS WILLIAMS
YEVGENY YEVTUSHENKO
MAO ZSEDONG

The Poems Listed Alphabetically

After an Anonymous Eighth-Century Gaelic Poet
Afterwords
Anasazi
Aphorism
A Tomos
Bard
Bestiary
Breton
Casa Grande
Closed Hearing
Dichotomy
Dylan's Walk
DT
Eyes
Figure of Jackson Mac Low
First Respects
Gwendolyn Reading in Black Voice
Hallelujah Man
Horizon
Janus
Lorca
Lorca's End
Movement in Voices
Randell Jarrell Went from Town
Riding on his Pony
R. Frost – Franconia, NH
Southern Draw
Southwest
The Golden Isles
To William Carlos Williams:
"In Memoriam"
Virtuosity

WRITERS
ON MY
WATCH

AFTER AN ANONYMOUS EIGHTH-CENTURY GAELIC POET

That long and cold day in Great Moor
foreshadowed devastating nights
with rain, no trifle, lashing through
the ancient wood that sheltered life,
the clean wind howling a great roar.

The gusts had broken his resolve,
had crushed the poet's spirit with
their great, relentless icy thrusts,
had drowned him in his human plight.
He suffered endlessly in time!

To voice his sad condition to the King,
(upon the distant star-bright throne),
like Job before his deity, who lacked
a sense of human suffering or need,
he wrote the pain in "Wind" and "Storm."

The poems shout of wind consuming life
like twigs beset by raging crimson fire
ordained by Heaven for a purpose that
the poet's reason cannot quite surmise.
There was no course but deep despair.

His grief took form in plaintive words
that still describe our meager state
(a hopeless fear yet shakes the mien
when Nature's elemental powers rear).
There is no respite from the cruel wind.

AFTERWORDS

On Mario Vargas Llosa

PEN AT PENN *February 14, 1991*

After words that Vargas Llosa & Oviedo said,
the Russian loomed up suddenly on stage--
quite tall & gaunt, with ruddy face & hair,
a raunchy tie of orange-red set off against
the jacket's camel hue--to take possession
of the honored guest and of our ears.

At dinner, Yevtushenko rambled on and on.
Directing his accented twang to Mario's face,
the table-hopping voice curtailed all speech
but his, its so-so Spanish nurtured years ago
in Castro's Cuba and Bolivia's heights,
where he had haunted Che Guevara's path.

Tyrant of the banquet table all night long,
he soon insisted that we clear away our talk
like dirty dishes and listen only to his voice
declaim a poem (in Spanish) he had written down
in honor of the Comandante's savage death
that fateful day when hunters felled their prey.

"A la izquierda, siempre a la izquierda," said
as he ranted from my right (his left, of course),
made his impassioned utterance first rise then fall
like the Bolivian hills where Che Guevara died.
The leftist words he'd spoken to the captors then
had nearly cost the Russian poet his own life.

Emphatic in recounting that old death, Yevgeny
placed Guevara's corpse where plates had been
(a somber Valentine) in front of dinner guests.
(A tired Vargas Llosa had retired to bed by then
and was not forced to witness how surrealistically
a fatuous symbiosis was attempted on that night.)

ANASAZI

For Tony Hillerman

The Old Ones
left the tribal land,
no trace about arroyos,
campgrounds, other sites,
no way to read
the footfalls of their trek.

The land was left
to die, alone

except for sherds
of their ceramic ware,

ladders that they climbed
to caves in cliffs,

the buried dead
and other bones,

the petroglyphs
on cavern walls,

the kivas of
their hallowed rites

the birth sipapu
bred on Mother Earth.

Their outward spiral
opened into time
and took them well beyond
their holy place
while yei whispered on
the remnant wind.

APHORISM

For Jorge Luis Borges

The blind man
is one from whom
the Universe
has been stolen
without redress
but for the
MIND'S EYE

A TOMOS

On Leucippus and Democritus

They are indivisible,
everlasting and thus,
in a persistent flow ...

We lose atoms
from the moment
of our birth

and being near inert
will not suffice
to curb the flow

too soon
we will be one
with all the universe
and cease to be
the one
that we have barely
known

BESTIARY

For Jorge Luis Borges

Ancient monsters,
degenerate and wild,
adorn the pages
in this exercise
of matter overcome
by mind's imaginings,
decadent with hard
illusions,
rampant stratagems

Behind the Beast
there lies the Beauty
that all things possess.

BRETON

On André Breton

BRETON.

A random thought in my antennae . . .
a moment of otherworldliness given precision
automatic processes bypassing ratiocination
unrelated simultaneities
hopscotch faces . . . names
umbilical cord nourishing all through
the athanor of the magus-alchemist-hierophant
through half-a-century-time
and distances of the world and universe
micro and macro together

UNISON.

CLOSED HEARING

On Howard Moss, reading ...

The words hang on the ears
like Spanish moss,
dangling, nearly lifeless
without feeling or innocence
intruding on one's expectations
with dank, loose greyness,
never quite touching,
hanging about fecklessly,
Moss having grown in years
within the schema of tall buildings
without a single bound
rather than on tree limbs
of some vital swamp
wherefrom it could hang
and mean

DICHOTOMY

For Jorge Luis Borges

I. A VERSION OF JUDAS

"I am a concept of the Son,
complex but logical,
therefore misinterpreted,
consequently, mankind's goat
the tragic sacrifice . . .

"I am excellent for conversation;
have me with your main course.

"I could have come as Pharaoh,
Mahomet, Alexander,
or the greatest Khan,
demolished all your kingdoms
and made the victory sign.

"If I had chosen,
Mormons could have been my people.
Or I could have been born
in black or brown with pinkish hands
riding backseat buses
yet, not man-deprived as I.

"I could have been made of laughter,
been a giraffe, prancing balletomane,
or a single tear
enough.

"I am ponderous yet.
I, Judas, chose to be myself.
I, Son of God,
Second in His Figure,
Redeemer!

"I was born a protestant;
I could have chosen to be
Christ.

      "God really dwells in Hell
      and I, Judas, stir the ashes
      resurrecting redemption
      for eternity."

II. SOLILOQUY

"I am Christ.
I hang upon my trestle cross
wondering your eyes can see,
having your spit and gall,
moving my hands on spikes.

"Your tribute words sing sky-round;
my veins disgorge pulsating blood.

"I am Christ,
and you have made my death
bearing me to Golgotha,
pounded to a cross,
panoramic,
mounted on a sea of skulls,
cadenced,
rippling the sky of storms.
"I am Christ,
a waking dead man of history
stirruped on a straddled mountain,
forced to serve
eternal."

DYLAN'S WALK

On Dylan Thomas

Above the estuary of Laugharne,
seeing gentle as the water rolled
ashore and out again to sea,
he strode on his high walks
with power of figure, mighty ken,
and rolling voice that carried,
like the tide, its own eternal gait.

Above the estuary of Laugharne,
poised within his flimsy wooden perch
[aerie for the eagle in the man],
he overlorded sea and land
and made them his through Bardic voice.

D T
On Dylan Thomas

He did not
go so gently
"into that
good night"

but drank
himself
into oblivion's
dark

instead of
burning, raving
on his
"close of day"

but then he
had not reached
"old age" as yet
and, taken
unaware
that Light
was spent,
he drank at bars
'til spirits
took his own
away

He had not raged
"against the dying
of the light"
for in his way
he knew that
"dark is right"
on that November
night.

EYES

For Jorge Luis Borges

Blind man,

blind man,

the star is black

the sun extinct

the moon eclipsed

    What demon

    has swallowed

    your light?

Blind man,

Blind man,

the star is near

the sun is harnessed

the moon is walked

    What god

    has stolen

    your mind?

FIGURE OF JACKSON MACLOW

You, sitting there
across four pieces of wood,
shaped,
wait the meantime
of the air-conditioner,
the espresso machine,
pulling your hair beard
away elastic face
to your breath.

You, whispered
in laughter in another across
abused and nervous
until yourself were an across
harsh in constrained bitterness
of defense--
excommunicated.

FIRST RESPECTS

On Mao Zedong

I hadn't thought of it at all.
The death had seemed to me
too far removed in many ways.

Yet, suddenly, I found myself
where large funereal wreaths
marked out a zone of sympathy
connected beyond space
to where the body lay
across the nautical
and the terrestrial miles.

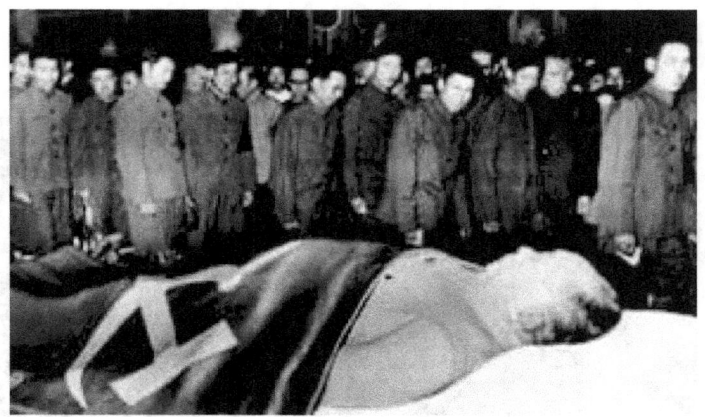

Mao's visage here
surrounded by real faces
of inscrutable demeanor
[yet heavy with the weight of loss]
expressing in their stillness
last respects.

The cadences of formal rites
the bows, the handshakes
the occasion to imbibe
the moment's silence
in the presence of a death
that will not die.

GWENDOLYN READING IN BLACK VOICE

On Gwendolyn Brooks

"Ugly" is bad enough
but she stretched it out in black,
deep in her gut, and
brought it to the surface,
making it rise up throaty:

Ü Ü Ü G ʻL I

The little boy in the poem
came alive through
her grave black voice
belching the ugliness he felt
when Black is supposed to be

B Ü ʻT I   F O O L

HALLELUJAH MAN

Leonard Cohen, In Memoriam

The worn fedora topping grizzled face
Of troubadour in grey, guitar in hand,
Whose shrouded voice sings of Suzanne
In a staccato chant of trials and tribulations,
And of love once had then lost
Pulsing into senses of the throng.

Bard of poetry & song,
The people clasp your cadences,
The raspy tone & smoky depth
That secret strife and secret night
Have given soul to voice of old
To thrill and to elate.
A perfect harmony of tune & word,
A hallelujah sound that tolls the bell
At break of day throughout the throes
Of sturm und drang endured
Through life's demanding trek
While angels back your plaint
With voices dulcet and demure.

A sadness throbs upon farewell
For you have etched
Your wisdom in flamenco riffs
But yet will sing upon your perch
A lasting paean to love and woes
In jazzy, bluesy notes at light's demise
within the tower of song.

Rest In Peace,
For everybody knows
Your voice will still resound,
Dancing to the end of love,
O Hallelujah Man!

HORIZON

For Jorge Luis Borges

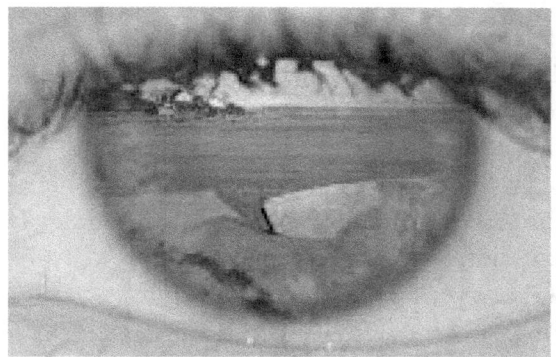

where the eye sees too far

where the mind thinks too large

matter shapeless, indistinct

beyond dimension or perspective

troglodytic and extinct

like the bloody sunset

JANUS

For Leroi Jones / Amiri Baraka

I
I remember you "back when,"

the Village as a setting for your shouts
of anger and disdain . . .
you being then among the loudest first
to cry out foul in voice and verse

the Sixties, in the Fuck You years,
before the anger metamorphosed
into guitar voice, and flower power
followed fists and clubs into the streets

You wore the name of king in that old time
but it didn't fit your rousing style,
the cause you battled to uphold
with words for actors and yourself

II
Today, you own a name with Africa inside.
And, in Dakar, I hear again your shouts,
your anger, your disdain and you are king,
as once before, but now it fits in this,
the continent where your ancestors live.

III
The old back home still use your early name.
To them you haven't changed, you said to me.
But you know that you've recomposed yourself--
become two poets now--looking, like the god,
in two directions, with two miens, at once
presiding over doors to old-time haunts
and gates that usher in the future wail.

LORCA.

On Federico García Lorca (1898-1936)

Eyes breaking
against paving stones
of ashen streets

Roots of the cry
in the mocking of
cacophony and spit

Syntax of sound
without cursive sense
terrible in its length
and cavernous depth

Soul moan into night
of torn flesh
and severed heart

Head rolling to and fro
on impact of the lead's
hot plunge,
the boot's emphatic thrust,
the coup-de-grace

No longer a matter of
time or place

Earth's entrails in red damp
unmarked, apart from identity

The solitude of neverness

LORCA'S END

Some words are mute
When they are confronted
 By the frigid night,
The arid night
Of the assassins

He died,
A Black Squad as his host
Led by an enemy of old,
A man whose lewdness
He did not caress

MOVEMENT IN VOICES

*Josif Brodskii, Reading
February 22, 1973*

Poems gifted without sense conveyed
reaching ears as epic song,
alien sound intrinsic in cadenzas
of a cantor's minstrelsy
Meaning sensed in body talk,
emboldened gestures, ritual mien,
orthodoxy's ancient liturgy
making theatre for the eyes

Utterance and movement meshed
to stir the deep resources,
just beyond the scheme of sense,
lying in the venue of the dream

RANDELL JARRELL WENT FROM TOWN RIDING ON HIS PONY

Randell Jarrell, Reading

At one moment
he was there
in life and big as
with his beard gone
(as he would be soon)
reading his poems
well and being a poem
sitting on the sofa
of a Hunter College
Bronx lounge

The next picture
has him with a coffee cup
and cookie crumbs,
a co-ed at each side
relishing and touching
seeking signatures
on their libidos

He autographed their books

The man loved it all
as poetry

R. FROST - FRANCONIA, NH

On Robert Frost

The flag is down beside your name,
painted folksily along the length
of your old battered box,
leaning slightly above knotty pole
(as once you must have rested there)
among wildflowers and the weeds.

No mail has been picked up,
delivered in these many years.
The flag is down beside your name:
a signal you're no longer here.

SOUTHERN DRAW

*For James Dickey
Columbia, S.C.
November 23, 1974*

I: Reception

Good ol' boy J.D.
bowing with rocky grace
kissing the hands of belles
relentlessly tremulous
in their décolletage
admiring his colossus
of a man

He was bigger than life
in his mint-julep setting
bourbon in hand
e   y   e   s
towering like beacons
sleeping
above the crowded room

II: Reading

He moved out loud
read with baited breath
as if he were tilting
at windmills
lurched emphatically
(recovered only slightly)
went on drawling Neruda
hip-shooter
with pin-ball moves
and mouthful words that stung
and a Jim Beam smile
the size of Carolina
that said hell was ok
if fair-haired was your game

III: Respite

In the end
it ended with relief
catharsis of applause
Good ol' boy J.D.
poet alive
carried it off
by the seat of his pants
with every possible hitch

SOUTHWEST

For Tony Hillerman

The Moon, one night from fullness,
witnessed the cold breath of Winter
riding roughshod in the pocket of Wind
over dark hills trembling without
the overcoat of their deciduous leaves.

Owl hooted.
Coyote bayed.
Bat winged.

Somewhere, Night carried an air
played by Kokopeli on his flute,
his silhouette bent into the dark
in curvature against the Moon,
the song heralding transcendence.

THE GOLDEN ISLES

For Ramón del Valle-Inclán

As old hexameters resound
with solar lust of gods and beasts,
and at the darkening of day,
when long-winged birds depart from marble ruins,
the wind resuscitates among last laurel trees
the calming murmur of Socratic fugues--
philosophy of stellar caste which transmigrated
out of myths and fables told relentlessly
within the span of man in time.

The tracks of the celestial bull
still lie upon the blue sea's edge.
The joyous songs are still becoming
in the shepherds' flutes of night.

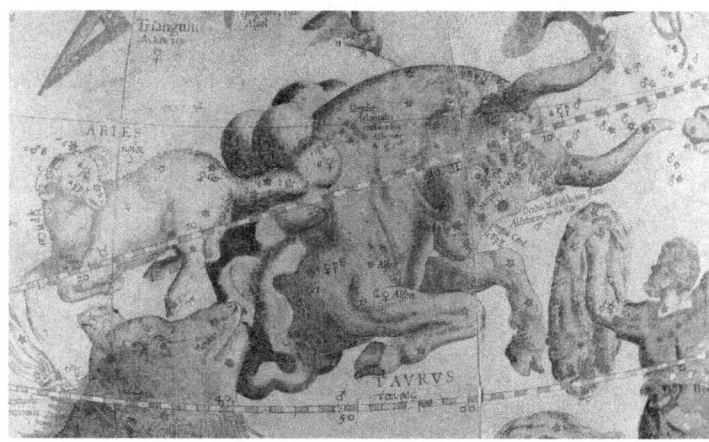

TO WILLIAM CARLOS WILLIAMS

"In Memoriam"

It is
your joy in having
still the thought--
"Our sons"--
in timelessness

Not as
new images of
your Paul,
your Bill,
but as
"Our younger,"
"Our elder"

And your
children's children
still,
as it should be,
"Our own"
is had
in your reality

Forever
should be
ours

VIRTUOSITY

On Paul West

Patience and Fortitude are virtues that define
the character of the man's whole life and work.

He fought with fierceness through the blatant
symptoms that encroached upon his mind,
denying access to his thoughts, to put in writing
the wondrous words he'd mastered all his life.

He kept his patience and with fortitude, stayed
in quietude as mind closed up and left him in
a nether place, where darkness reigned, adrift
beyond the pale where words became delusional.

Roiling and detained in passage, astir, his
words were fighting through to utterance.

And so, when rare lucidity allowed him to express
his voice, he told his scribe the story that he'd held.
It was a tale of the privation and frustration felt
when mental faculties were shackled into absence.

This tale was different from his previous prose,
venting bizarre thoughts obscurity had prompted
that cast upon him spells of separation, otherness,
leaving but a state of vacancy, bereft of self.

Patience and Fortitude are the guardian lions
that define the staircase to the main library's gates.
And as they guard the world of books, himself
become a Literary Lion, is virtually enshrined.

About the Author

ROBERT LIMA is a Cuban-born award-winning poet, and an internationally-recognized critic, bibliographer, playwright, and translator. He retired after 40 years in the teaching profession as Professor Emeritus of Spanish and Comparative Literatures at The Pennsylvania State University, as well as Fellow Emeritus of the Institute for the Arts and Humanistic Studies. Previously, he had taught at Hunter College, CUNY, and abroad in Perú and Cameroon, lecturing widely in the U.S. and overseas.

He earned the B.A. in English (1957) and the M.A. in Theatre and Drama (1961) at Villanova University. His Ph.D. in Romance Languages and Literatures was awarded in 1968 (GSAS) with departmental honors by New York University, which also presented him The Founders Day Award. At NYU, he was fortunate to have had three prominent figures as his professors: Francisco Ayala, Joaquín Casalduero and Ernesto Da Cal.

He is an Academician of the Academia Norteamericana de la Lengua Española and a Corresponding Member of the Real Academia Española. He has been honored as a Distinguished Alumnus by Villanova University, inducted into the Enxebre Orden da Vieira in Spain, initiated in Phi Kappa Phi, and named Knight Commander in the Order of Queen Isabel of Spain by His Majesty King Juan Carlos I. A second knighthood, in the Imperial Hispanic Order of Charles V, was bestowed on him at The Alcázar in Segovia, Spain, by the His Serene Highness, the Prince of Borbón.

Among his numerous books are *The Theatre of García Lorca* (Las Américas, 1963), *Ramón del Valle-Inclán* (Columbia UP, 1972), *An Annotated Bibliography of Valle-Inclán* (Penn State U. Libraries, 1972), *Dos ensayos sobre teatro español de los veinte* (U. de Murcia, 1984), and *Valle-Inclán. The Theatre of His Life* (Missouri UP, 1988). He has translated Valle-Inclán's aesthetico-mystical treatise *The Lamp of Marvels* (Lindisfarne Press, 1986) and his selection of short dramas *Savage Acts: Four Plays* (Estreno, 1993). Other recent books are *Dark Prisms. Occultism in Hispanic Drama* (UP of Kentucky, 1995; also in paperback, 2009) and *Valle-Inclán. El teatro de su vida* (Editorial Nigra, Spain, 1995), *Ramón del Valle-Inclán: An Annotated Bibliography* (Grant & Cutler, 1999), *The Dramatic World of Valle-Inclán* (Boydell & Brewer, 2003), *Stages of Evil. Occultism in Western Theatre and Drama* (UP of Kentucky), published in 2005, and *The International Bibliography of Studies on the Life and Works of Ramón del Valle-Inclán* (Orlando Press, 2008). The Spanish version of *Dark Prisms* was published in 2010 in Madrid by Editorial Fundamentos. *Words of Power. Adages, Axioms and Aphorisms* was published in California by Floricanto Press, while his memoir *¡Some People! Anecdotes, Images and Letters of Persons of Interest* appeared in 2015, as did *Provenance and Residuals. Bringing the Past Forward*, his autobiography. His newest books are *Ikons of the Past. Poetry of the Hispanic Americas* (2018) and *Across the Spectrum. Hispanic Cultural Heritage* (2019). His new book of poetry is *Elementals* (2019).

He selected for publication, edited, and translated Barrenechea's *Borges the Labyrinth Maker* (NYU Press, 1965), the first critical study on Borges in English, as well as edited and contributed to *Borges and the Esoteric*, a special issue of *Crítica Hispánica* (Duquesne UP, 1993). Also, he has published well over one hundred fifty refereed articles in a variety of fields.

In 1974, he created "Surrealism--A Celebration," a multi-faceted event in honor of the 50th anniversary of the Surrealist Movement. Included were theatre productions, music concerts, films, displays of rare publications, paintings, sculpture, jewelry and other objects, presentations by leading art historians, artists, and literary critics. And a Surrealist banquet. Elements of these events appeared in a special 1975 issue of *Journal of General Education*, which he edited

Over six hundred of his poems have appeared throughout the U.S. and abroad in periodicals, anthologies, and in his poetry collections *Fathoms* (1981), *The Olde Ground* (1985), *Mayaland* (1992), *Sardinia / Sardegna* (2000), *Tracking the Minotaur* (2003), *The Pointing Bone* (2008*), The Rites of Stone* (2010), *Self* (2012), *Por caminos errantes* (2014), *Celestials* (2017), *Cancionería Cubana* (2017), *Ikons of the Past. Poetry of the Hispanic Americas* (2018), and *Elementals* (2019). *Poems of Exile and Alienation* (with Teresinka Pereira, 1976) and *Corporal Works* (1985) are two of his chapbooks. From 1959 to 1965, he was involved in the New York City poetry movement, reading throughout Greenwich Village and the East Village with such as David Ignatow, Paul Blackburn, Diana Wakoski, Denise Levertov, Robert Kelly, et. al.

He has been elected to membership in PEN International and the Poetry Society of America. From March through August 2004, Penn State University Libraries exhibited "The Poetic World of Robert Lima," a retrospective of his poetry career from 1955 to that year. The first poetry competition by Phi Kappa Phi was won by his poem "Astrals," which appears in the honor society's journal *Forum*. Another major exhibit of his poetry was "Word and Image:

The Poetry of Robert Lima," held at The Bellefonte Art Museum in conjunction with April, National Poetry Month, in 2017. He was invited to record his poetry in Spanish and English at The Library of Congress Hispanic Division, joining such luminaries as Jorge Luis Borges, Mario Vargas Llosa, Octavio Paz, and Gabriel Garcia Márquez, among others, in the LOC Archive.

His biography appears in *Who's Who in the World*, *Who's Who in America*, *Who's Who in the East*, *World Who's of Authors,* and in other international and national directories.